"SHE WAS THE QUEEN OF DISCO,"
SAID LIZA MINNELLI.
"WE WILL BE DANCING TO HER MUSIC FOREVER."

DONNA SUMMER

DONNA SUMMER

CHAPTER 1:
I Remember Yesterday

DONNA SUMMER PASSED ON MAY 17, 2012, AFTER BATTLING LUNG CANCER.

BOOM

DESPITE SMOKING SOME WELL BEFORE FAME SHOT HER TO THE TOP OF THE CHARTS, DONNA WAS BAFFLED BY HER DIAGNOSIS.

SHE BELIEVED HER CANCER WAS CAUSED BY INHALING TOXIC FUMES AND THICK DUST IN THE WAKE OF THE SEPTEMBER 11, 2001, ATTACKS ON THE TWIN TOWERS IN NEW YORK.

HER APARTMENT WAS CLOSE TO GROUND ZERO. IN THE DAYS FOLLOWING THE ATTACK, SHE WAS PARANOID ABOUT THE DUST.

SHE HUNG SILK SHEETS IN HER DRESSING ROOM AND OFTEN SPRAYED DISINFECTANT INTO THE AIR.

BRIAN EDWARD, A REPRESENTATIVE FOR HER FAMILY, RELEASED A STATEMENT ABOUT HER DIAGNOSIS THAT READ, IN PART:

"OBVIOUSLY, NUMEROUS FACTORS CAN BE ATTRIBUTED TO THE CAUSE OF CANCER IN GENERAL, BUT ANY DETAILS REGARDING THE DIAGNOSIS AND SUBSEQUENT TREATMENT OF MS. SUMMER'S CASE REMAIN BETWEEN HER FAMILY AND TEAM OF DOCTORS."

CHAPTER 2:
Heaven Knows

LADONNA ADRIAN GAINES
WAS BORN IN BOSTON,
MASSACHUSETTS,
ON DECEMBER 31, 1948,
AND RAISED IN
THE NEIGHBORHOOD
OF MISSION HILL.

AMAZING GRACE,
HOW SWEET
THE SOUND THAT
SAVED A WRETCH
LIKE ME.

THE THIRD OF SEVEN CHI
WAS RAISED IN TH

HER FATHER,
ANDREW GAINES,
WAS A BUTCHER
WHO SERVED
AS A MINISTER,
INSTILLING A
WORKING-CLASS
SENSIBILITY
AND A RESPECT
FOR RELIGION
IN HIS CHILDREN.

MARY, HER MOTHER, WAS A
WHO REINFORCED THE IMF
OF EDUCATION IN LADON

GROWING UP IN A CROWDED HOUSEHOLD,
LADONNA OFTEN SANG WITH HER SISTERS
TO ENTERTAIN THEMSELVES.

LIVING IN SERVICE TO GOD IN A MIDDLE-CLASS NEIGHBORHOOD MEANT THAT THE FAMILY WASN'T RICH, BUT LADONNA DIDN'T NEED MATERIAL TRAPPINGS.

"I HAVE AN INCREDIBLE ABILITY TO FANTASIZE – I REALLY DO. I DON'T HAVE TO HAVE THINGS TANGIBLE TO BE ABLE TO SEE THEM, AND THEREFORE I ENJOY SO MANY THINGS BECAUSE THEY'RE IN MY MIND," SHE TOLD AN INTERVIEWER.

"BUT I THINK I'M JUST A NORMAL GIRL, YOU KNOW?"

HI. CAN YOU INTRODUCE YOURSELF?

LADONNA GAINES.

CHAPTER 3:
Try Me, I Know We can Make It
CASTING

ON YOUR RESUME, YOU MENTION THAT YOUR EXPERIENCE IS SINGING IN CHURCH, IN HIGH SCHOOL CHOIRS, AND A BLUES-ROCK BAND NAMED –

CROW. YEAH. THEY NEEDED A FEMALE SINGER, SO... THEY GOT ME.

TELL ME ABOUT THAT.

ABOUT CROW?

WELL, WE THOUGHT WE WERE GONNA LAND A RECORDING CONTRACT —

WE WERE SO CLOSE! — SO, I MOVED HERE. I GUESS GOD HAD OTHER PLANS.

I'M QUITE THE BELTER.

"I SEE. WE'RE LOOKING TO REPLACE MELBA MOORE IN HAIR."

"BIG SHOES TO FILL."

YEAH... BIG SHOES BIGGER VOICE.

"OKAY! LET'S HEAR IT."

"I LEARNED HOW TO PROJECT WHEN I WAS VERY YOUNG.

I WAS A NATURAL FOR THE THEATER."

LADONNA WAS CAST IN THE COUNTERCULTURE MUSICAL HAIR, JOINING THE TROUPE FOR THEIR TOUR OF EUROPE.

HER RELIGIOUS UPBRINGING SEEMED AT ODDS WITH THE MESSAGES – AND THE COSTUMES – PRESENTED IN THE LAVISH STAGE PRODUCTION.

IT TOOK A LOT TO CONVINCE HER STRICT, DEVOUT FATHER TO LET HER GO WITH THE PRODUCTION TO THEIR DATES IN GERMANY.

"I GREW UP IN A CLEAN, PRISTINE ENVIRONMENT. SO, SAYING A CURSE WORD WAS AS BAD AS IT GOT."

THE TOUR WOULD TAKE THEM TO GERMANY, SO LADONNA LEARNED THE SONGS IN GERMAN WITHOUT UNDERSTANDING THEM.

IT WASN'T UNTIL SHE WAS MUCH OLDER THAT SHE LEARNED THE ENGLISH VERSION OF THE SONGS.

"MY GOD, WAS THAT I WAS SINGING ABOUT?"

DONNA FELL IN LOVE WITH HER NEW LIFE IN GERMANY, EVENTUALLY LEARNING THE LANGUAGE AND IMMERSING HERSELF IN THE CULTURE.

I DON'T SPEAK GERMAN VERY WELL - BUT I CAN TRY IF YOU LIKE!

DONNA WOULD STAY IN GERMANY FOR FIVE YEARS AFTER HER GIG WITH HAIR ENDED, JOINING THE VIENNESE FOLK OPERA AND PERFORMING IN MUSICALS SUCH AS SHOWBOAT,

... PORGY & BESS:

...AND GODSPELL.

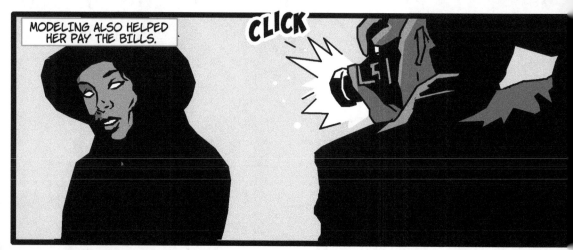

MODELING ALSO HELPED HER PAY THE BILLS.

CLICK

DURING A VACATION IN SWITZERLAND, LADONNA MET AND FELL IN LOVE WITH AUSTRIAN ACTOR HELMUTH SOMMER.

THEY MARRIED IN 1972.

"MY LIFE WAS CHANGED IN ONE BREATH FROM GOD," SHE SAID.

A YEAR LATER, THEY WOULD WELCOME THEIR DAUGHTER MIMI.

THANK YOU, MAMMA.

AUF WIEDERSEHEN, KIND. ICH LIEBE DICH.

IT WAS A CHALLENGING TIME FOR LADONNA, WHO STAYED WITH HELMUTH'S PARENTS IN VIENNA WHILE WORKING LONG HOURS.

"GOD DID NOT MAKE ME STRONG ENOUGH TO DO THAT."

"I WANT TO BE ABLE TO KNOW THAT IF I GET TIRED, SOMEBODY IS THERE TO HOLD UP THE FORT."

"I LIKE TO KNOW THAT SOMEONE IS STRONGER THAN I AM."

CHAPTER 4:
State of Independence

IN 1974, DONNA WORKED AS A VOCALIST FOR MUSICLAND STUDIOS IN GERMANY, LAYING BACKGROUND TRACKS FOR THREE DOG NIGHT.

HER POWERFUL VOICE ATTRACTED ATTENTION.

PETE, YOU'VE REALLY GOTTA HEAR THIS.

MAN OH? WHAT IS IT, MATE?

DAMN. IMPRESSIVE.

YEAH, I KEEP PULLING HER DOWN. SHE'S OVERPOWERING THE OTHERS.

GIORGIO!

LET HIM HEAR THIS.

GIORGIO MORODER

FOUNDER, OASIS RECORDS

SHE SIGNED WITH OASIS RECORDS.

THE FIRST SINGLE, "HOSTAGE," WAS RELEASED EXCLUSIVELY IN THE NETHERLANDS AS PART OF HER DEBUT ALBUM, LADY OF THE NIGHT, IN JUNE OF 1974.

THE 7-INCH SINGLE WAS ISSUED IN EUROPE AND ASIA A FEW MONTHS LATER.

IT WOULD TAKE NORTH AMERICA BY STORM A YEAR LATER.

IN "HOSTAGE," DONNA PLAYS A WOMAN WHOSE HUSBAND WAS KIDNAPPED. THE SONG'S LYRICS WOULD PROVE CONTROVERSIAL.

THE MOST HIGHLY FOLLOWED KIDNAPPING CASES IN FBI HISTORY OCCURRED ON FEBRUARY 4, 1974. A GROUP OF MEN AND WOMEN FROM THE SYMBIONESE LIBERATION ARMY, LED BY DONALD DEFREEZE, KNOCKED ON THE DOOR TO PATTY HEARST'S APARTMENT.

KNOCK. KNOCK KNOCK.

HELLO? I... OH!

THEY BURST IN, ASSAULTED HER FIANCÉ, AND KIDNAPPED PATTY, STOWING HER IN THE TRUNK OF A CAR.

FOR THE NEXT TWO MONTHS, THE SLA KEPT PATTY BLINDFOLDED IN THEIR HEADQUARTERS, RELEASING TAPES TO THE MEDIA THAT ASKED FOR MILLIONS OF DOLLARS IN FOOD DONATIONS IN EXCHANGE FOR HER FREEDOM.

PLEASE... LISTEN TO ME! WHAT DO YOU WANT? I'M NOT WHO YOU'RE LOOKING FOR!

PLEASE! I...

SHHH!

SHE FELT HELPLESS DURING THIS TIME. SHE WOULD LATER TELL AUTHORITIES THAT HER TORTURE ESCALATED. SHE CLAIMED SEXUAL AND PSYCHOLOGICAL ABUSE AND LONG BOUTS OF ISOLATION.

OVER TIME, SHE GREW TO IDENTIFY WITH THE SLA AND THEIR IDEOLOGY.

MY NAME IS TANIA, AND I AM A SOLDIER OF THE PEOPLE'S ARMY.

ON MAY 16, SLA MEMBERS WERE CAUGHT IN THE ACT OF STEALING AMMUNITION FROM A STORE IN LOS ANGELES.

BANG

THE POLICE CHASED THEM TO THEIR SAFEHOUSE. THE SHOOTOUT CAUSED THE BUILDING TO ERUPT IN FLAMES.

SIX SLA MEMBERS DIED, SCATTERING THE REST ACROSS THE COUNTRY.

WHEN THE FBI CAUGHT UP WITH PATTY, THEY ARRESTED HER FOR BANK ROBBERY AND OTHER CRIMES.

FBI   SAN FRANCISCO
PATRICIA
CAMPBELL
HEARST
SEPT 18 1975

HER TRIAL WAS A SENSATION, WITH FAMOUS LITIGATOR F. LEE BAILEY DEFENDING HER, CLAIMING STOCKHOLM SYNDROME AS A DEFENSE.

SHE WAS SENTENCED TO TWO YEARS IN PRISON, BUT PRESIDENT JIMMY CARTER COMMUTED IT.

I MEAN, THEY CALL IT STOCKHOLM SYNDROME AND POST-TRAUMATIC STRESS DISORDER. AND, YOU KNOW, I HAD NO FREE WILL. I HAD VIRTUALLY NO FREE WILL UNTIL I WAS SEPARATED FROM THEM FOR ABOUT TWO WEEKS.

"HOSTAGE" SEEMED TO CAPITALIZE ON THE SENSATIONAL NATURE OF THE HEARST STORY AND, THOUGH A FEW MONTHS AFTER THE SONG'S RELEASE, THE FATE OF BERLIN POLITICIAN GÜNTER VON DRENKMANN, KIDNAPPED AND KILLED DURING THE ATTEMPT ON NOVEMBER 10, 1974, RESONATED.

THE SONG WAS REMOVED FROM GERMAN AIRWAVES AND...

THEY SPELLED MY NAME WRONG. "SUMMER"? REALLY?

The Hostage
L'Otage Donna Summer

HER NEW NAME, HOWEVER, WOULD STICK AROUND FOR A WHILE.

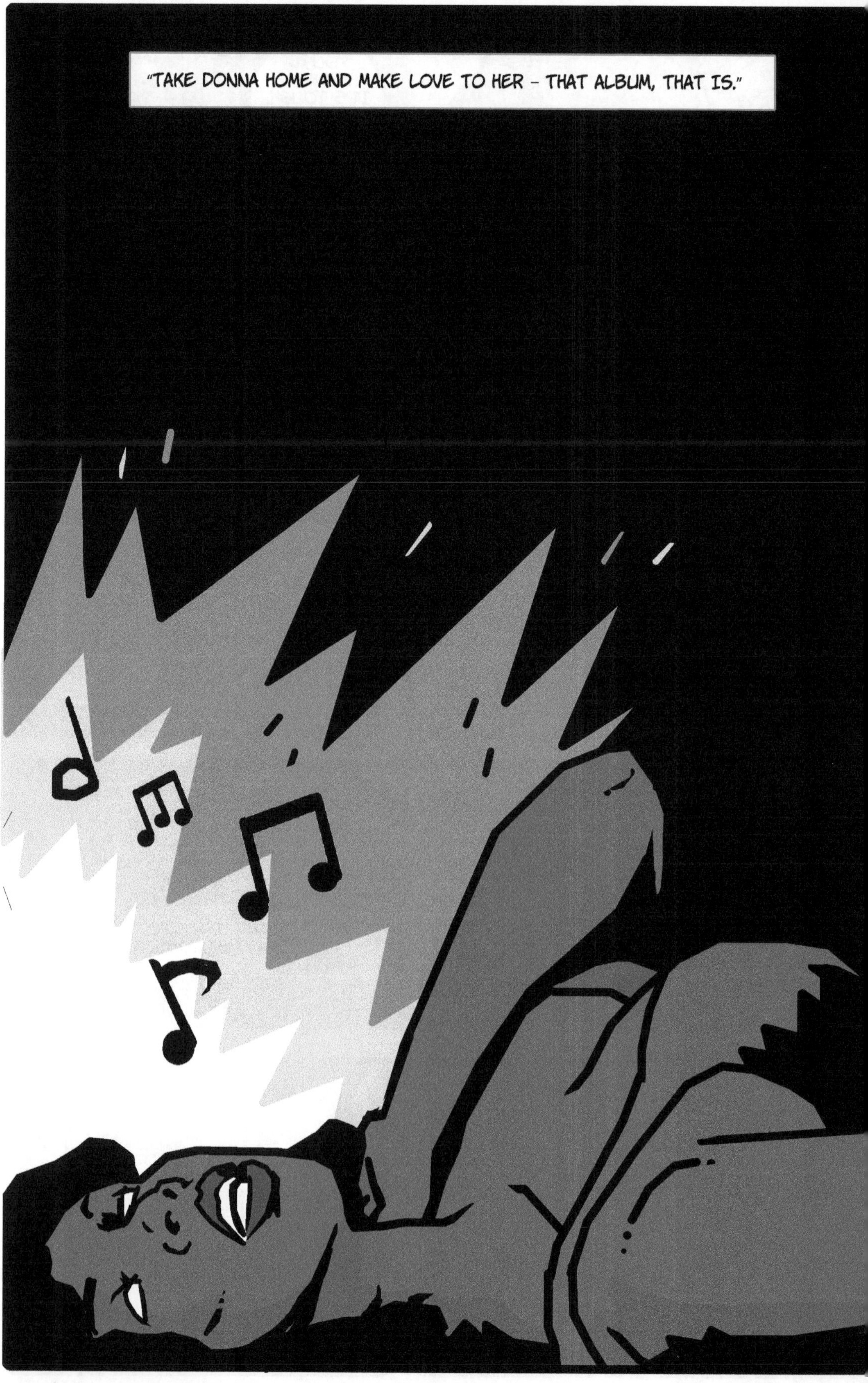
"TAKE DONNA HOME AND MAKE LOVE TO HER – THAT ALBUM, THAT IS."

NEIL BOGART
CASABLANCA
RECORDS

WAIT... WHAT?

WE'LL BUY IT AND RECORD IT, BUT I WANT A BEAUTIFUL, GREAT BALLING RECORD. I WANT PEOPLE TO FEEL LIKE THEY'RE TAKING DONNA HOME AND MAKING LOVE TO HER.

"WE'LL ASK RADIO STATIONS TO PLAY THE TRACK AT MIDNIGHT. IT'LL SPARK SOME ROMANCE, KNOW WHAT I'M SAYING?"

"MAKE IT FEEL DANGEROUS, LIKE THE SOUNDTRACK TO AN ORGY.

"EXTEND THE SONG. PROLONG RELEASE, IF YOU KNOW WHAT I MEAN."

DID YOU GET IT? DID YOU FEEL IT?

WE CAN DO THAT, RIGHT?

"LOVE TO LOVE YOU BABY" BECAME A 16-MINUTE EPIC WITH DONNA MOANING 22 RECORDED "ORGASMS."

CHAPTER 7:
Finger on the Trigger

BOGART'S PLAN WORKED, AND THE SONG SWEPT THE NATION IN 1975 AT THE HEIGHT OF DISCO'S INFLUENCE.

THE INTERPLAY BETWEEN DANCE GROOVES AND RAW SEXUALITY EXPLODED ON THE CLUB SCENE.

"DANCE MUSIC DOESN'T CARE WHERE YOU LIVE. IT DOESN'T CARE WHO YOUR FRIENDS ARE".

"IT DOESN'T CARE HOW MUCH MONEY YOU MAKE. IT DOESN'T CARE IF YOU'RE 74 OR IF YOU ARE 24 BECAUSE... 74 IS THE NEW 24!" GIORGIO SAID IN AN INTERVIEW ABOUT THE TIME FOLLOWING DONNA'S METEORIC RISE.

FIVE MINUTES, MS. SUMMER.

"ONCE YOU FREE YOUR MIND ABOUT A CONCEPT OF MUSIC AND HARMONY BEING CORRECT,

YOU CAN DO WHATEVER YOU WANT."

LADIES AND GENTLEMEN: DONNA SUMMER!

"I DON'T LIKE BEING CALLED THE GODFATHER OF DISCO AND ELECTRONIC MUSIC. IT'S BETTER THAN BEING CALLED THE GRANDFATHER, BUT I STILL DON'T LIKE IT," GIORGIO WOULD LATER TELL *THE GUARDIAN*.

BETWEEN 1976 AND 1978, DONNA WOULD EARN FOUR GOLD RECORDS.

SONGS "I FEEL LOVE" AND "BAD GIRLS" CEMENTED HER STATUS AS THE DISCO QUEEN.

BUT SUCCESS PROVED BITTERSWEET AS DONNA STRUGGLED WITH HER IMAGE AND THE LACK OF PERSONAL CONTROL OVER HER LIFE. SHE SUFFERED FROM DARK BOUTS OF DEPRESSION, LEANING ON HER FAITH TO SUSTAIN HER.

BY 1983, DONNA HAD RELEASED TEN ALBUMS, REMADE HER DISCO QUEEN IMAGE WITH HER SELF-TITLED 1982 ALBUM, AND GRAMMY NOMINATIONS FOR "LOVE IS IN CONTROL (FINGER ON THE TRIGGER)."

CHAPTER 8:
The Woman in Me

"WE WERE AT A PARTY FOR JULIO IGLESIAS AT CHASEN'S RESTAURANT IN BEVERLY HILLS IN 1982. I REMEMBER STRUGGLING AT THIS POINT IN MY CAREER. I WAS TIRED, AND IDEAS WEREN'T COMING LIKE THEY USED TO.

DO YOU HEAR THAT?

YEAH, I THINK... I DON'T KNOW.

IT SOUNDS LIKE A T.V. SET.

"HEARING THE SOUND, I THOUGHT, 'HOW POSH! THIS PLACE HAS A T.V. IN THE BATHROOM.'

"I DIDN'T EXPECT THIS.

"SHE WAS JUST GONE — SHE WAS ASLEEP. AND THE T.V. WAS JUST BLASTING.

"I LOOKED AT HER, AND MY HEART JUST FILLED UP WITH COMPASSION FOR THIS LADY, I THOUGHT,

'GOD, SHE WORKS HARD FOR THE MONEY, COOPED UP IN THIS STINKY LITTLE ROOM ALL NIGHT.'"

"TURNS OUT SHE HAD. SHE WORKED AN EIGHT-HOUR SHIFT AT A HOSPITAL AND ANOTHER FOUR AT CHASEN'S. IT WAS 2:30 A.M.!"

SUSAN! SHE WORKS HARD FOR THE MONEY! THIS IS IT! THIS IS IT! I KNOW THIS IS IT.

"I DON'T REALLY TRY TO PREDICT WHAT CAN AND WILL HAPPEN WITH THINGS. SOMETIMES YOU THINK SOMETHING'S GONNA BE A HUGE SUCCESS, AND IT

"AND SOMETIMES YOU PAY NO ATTENTION TO SOMETHING WHATSOEVER, AND GOD JUST MAKES IT INTO EVERYTHING."

"SHE WORKS HARD FOR THE MONEY" WAS A RUNAWAY SUCCESS, REACHING #15 ON THE BILLBOARD HOT 100 CHART.

ONETTA LATER TOLD THE DAILY NEWS:

"I WAS SAYING TO MYSELF, 'WHY DON'T THESE PEOPLE GO HOME?' I HAD TO TAKE A NURSING EXAM THE NEXT DAY. EVERY SO OFTEN, WE HAVE TO REVIEW OUR WORK TO KEEP OUR LICENSE."

DONNA MADE SURE ONETTA RECEIVED CREDIT.

ONETTA

"GOD HAD TO CREATE DISCO MUSIC SO I COULD BE BORN AND BE SUCCESSFUL,"

DONNA TOLD AN INTERVIEWER.

AS HER CAREER WANED IN THE TWILIGHT YEARS OF THE 80S, DONNA TURNED HER ATTENTION TO PAINTING, GARNERING PRAISE – AND CRITICISM.

"YOU'VE GOT TO MAINTAIN YOUR LEVEL OF SELF-ESTEEM THROUGH EVERYTHING. YOU ARE WHO YOU ARE, AND NOBODY WILL EVER BE ABLE TO TAKE THAT FROM YOU IF YOU DON'T LET THEM."

DONNA WOULD FALL IN LOVE WITH BRUCE SUDANO HAVE TWO MORE DAUGHTERS.

"NOBODY WANTS YOU TO STOP, OBVIOUSLY BECAUSE YOU'RE A MONEYMAKING MACHINE. BUT YOU HAVE TO MAKE THE DECISION, AND YOU HAVE TO MOVE FORWARD. SO, I TOOK TIME OFF TO HAVE BABIES AND DO ALL THAT."

TIDALWAVE
COMICS

Michael Frizell — Writer

Victor Moura — Art

Pablo Martinena — Letters

Darren G. Davis — Editor

Pablo Martinena — Cover

Cover B: Ramon Salas

Darren G. Davis
Publisher

Maggie Jessup
Publicity

Susan Ferris
Entertainment Manager

Steven Diggs Jr.
Marketing Manager

Lightning Source UK Ltd.
Milton Keynes UK
UKHW051936110522
402829UK00002B/35